Yoga with Santa

Marcy Schaaf

It's the most magical time of the year, and Santa is busy preparing for his big Christmas Eve journey! But delivering presents all over the world is a lot of work, and this year, Santa wants to make sure he's ready in a whole new way.

Join Santa as he discovers the joy of yoga, stretching and moving to get himself ready for his busiest night. With help from Mrs. Claus and the elves, Santa learns that a little flexibility, balance, and fun can go a long way–especially when it comes to spreading holiday cheer!

Let's roll out our mats and do some Yoga with Santa!

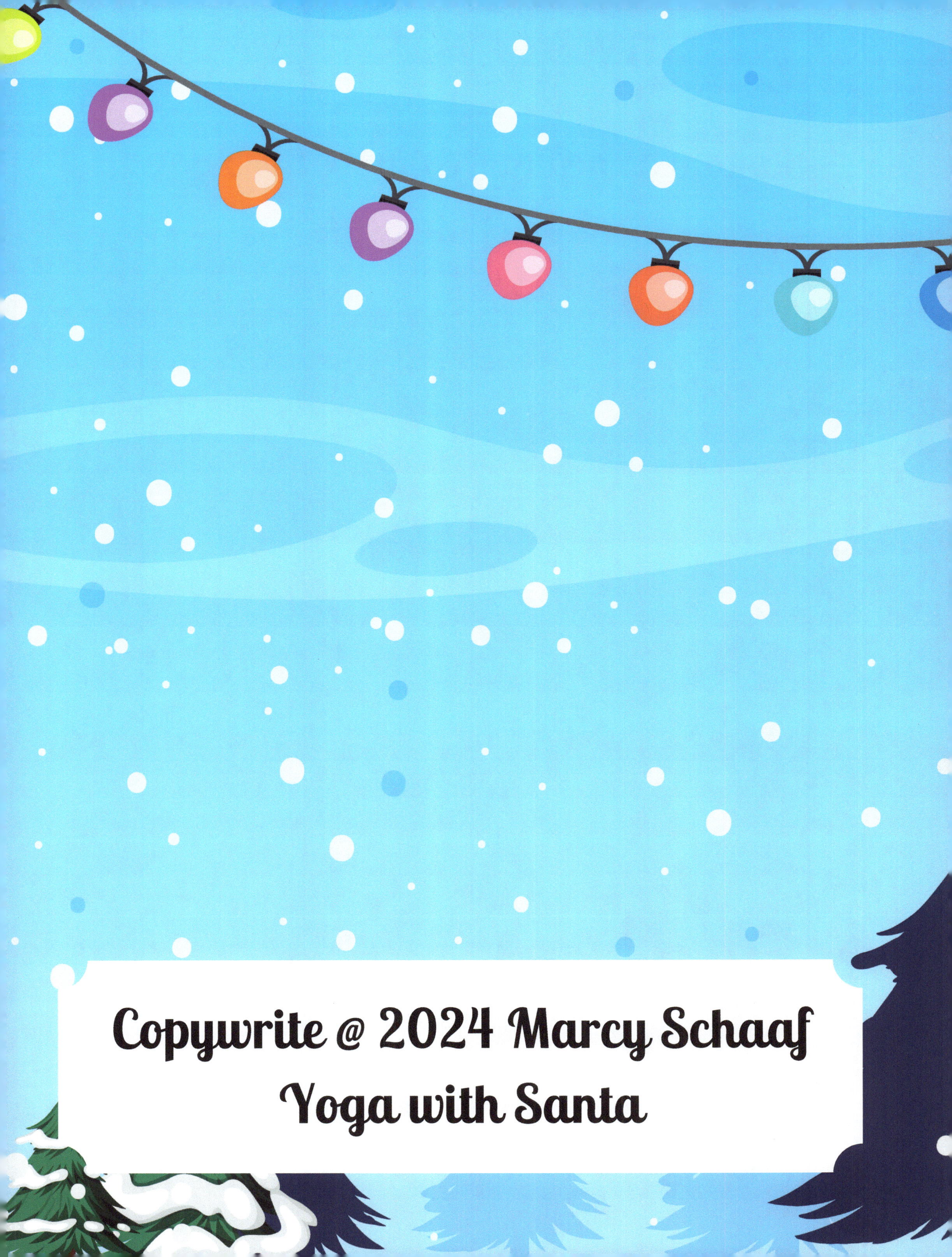

Santa was getting ready for his biggest
night of the year.

But this year, Santa felt a bit stiff from sitting all day.

Mrs. Claus said "Yoga will make you feel flexible and strong again!"

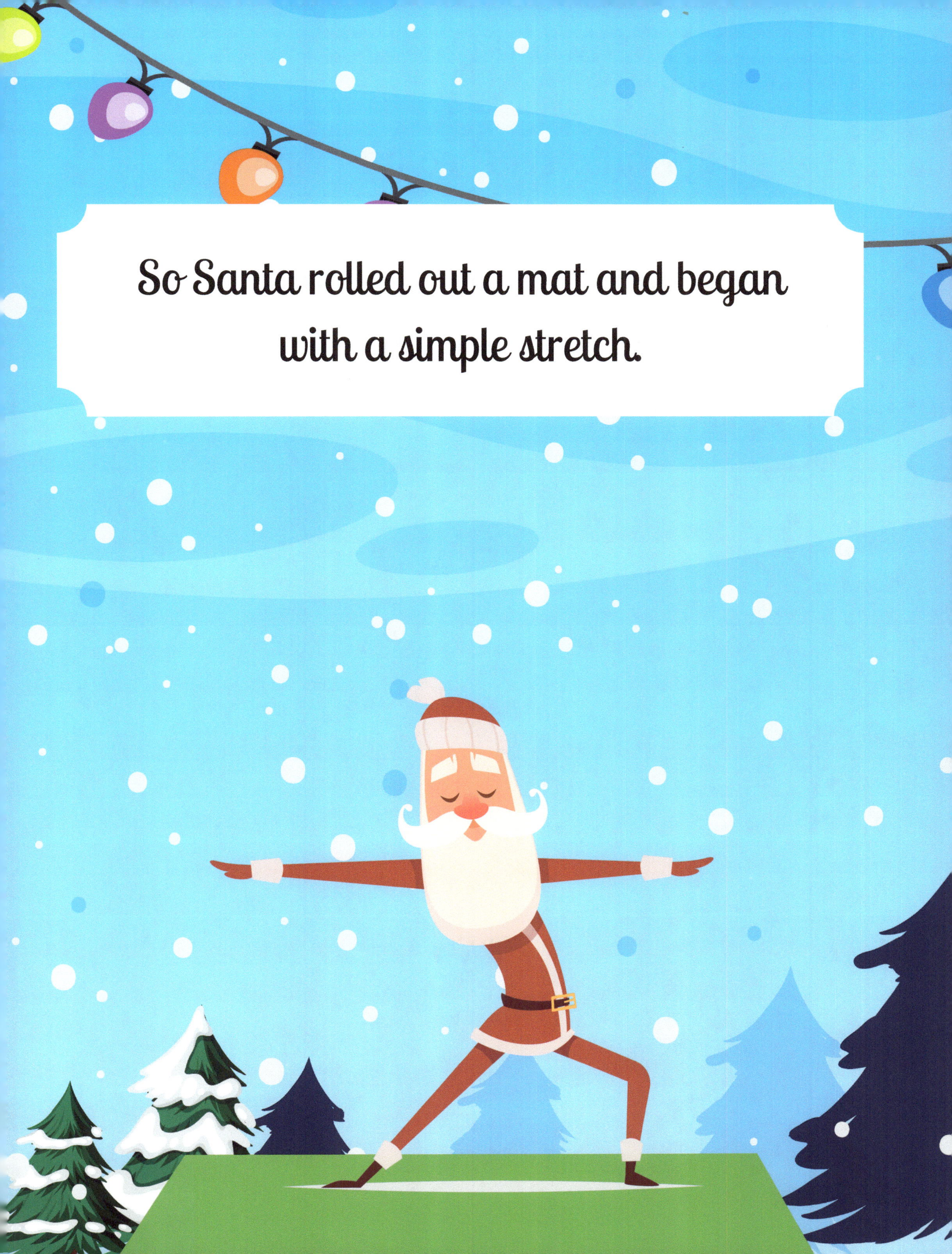

So Santa rolled out a mat and began
with a simple stretch.

First, Santa reached his arms high,
stretching toward the North Star.

Next, Santa bent down, touching his toes
like a candy cane.

He then twisted his waist like a pretzel.
"Feeling looser already!"

Santa balanced on one leg, pretending to be a tall Christmas tree.

"Whoa!" he said, wobbling a little, "This is harder than I thought!"

Santa did the reindeer pose, crouching low and stretching his back.

"Dasher and Dancer always so quick—
maybe this will help us too!"

Prancer lifted his arms, pretending to fly like his sleigh in the night sky.

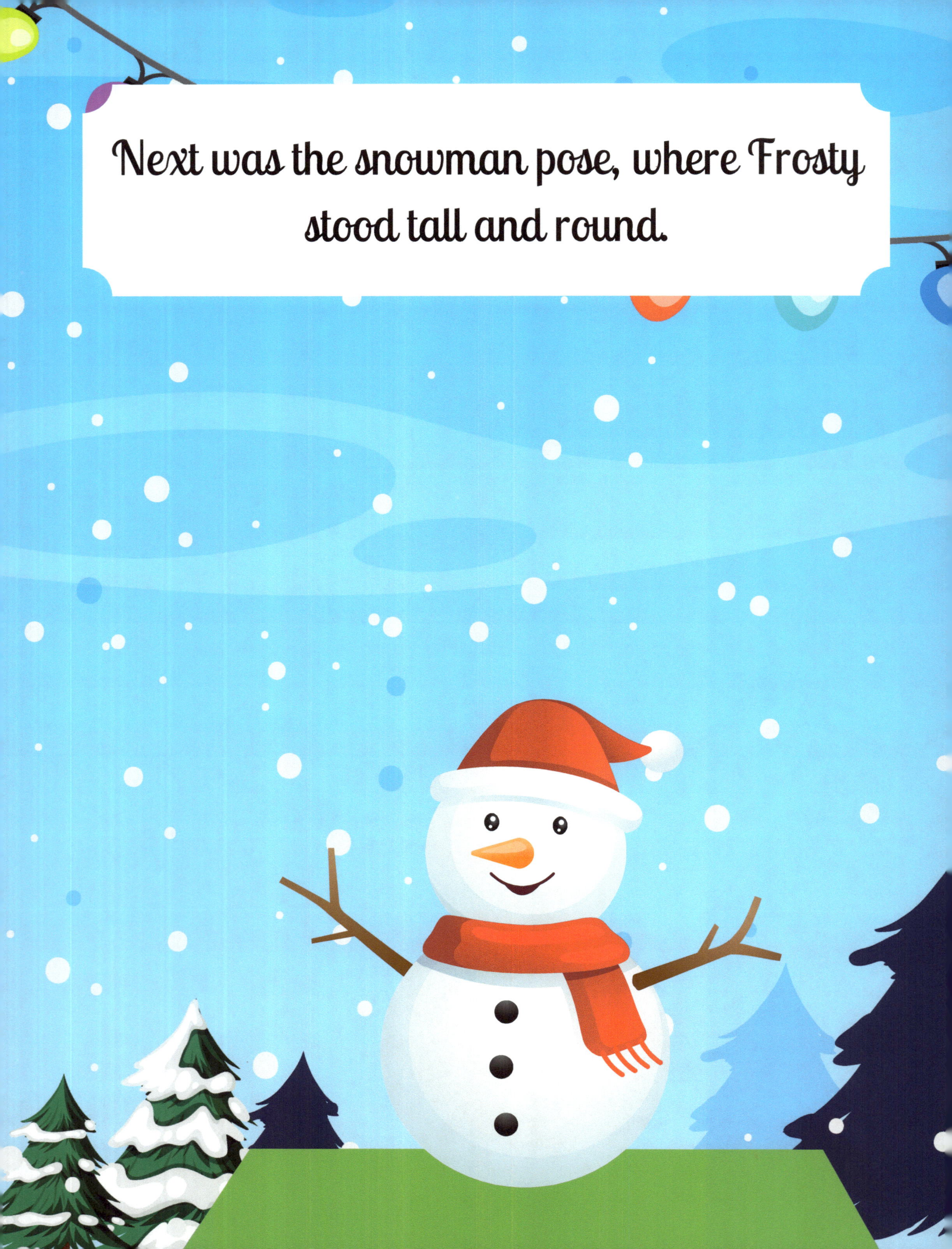

Next was the snowman pose, where Frosty stood tall and round.

"Ho ho ho!" Santa laughed.
"Look at Frosty!"

"I feel great!" Santa said.
"I'm ready to take on Christmas Eve!"

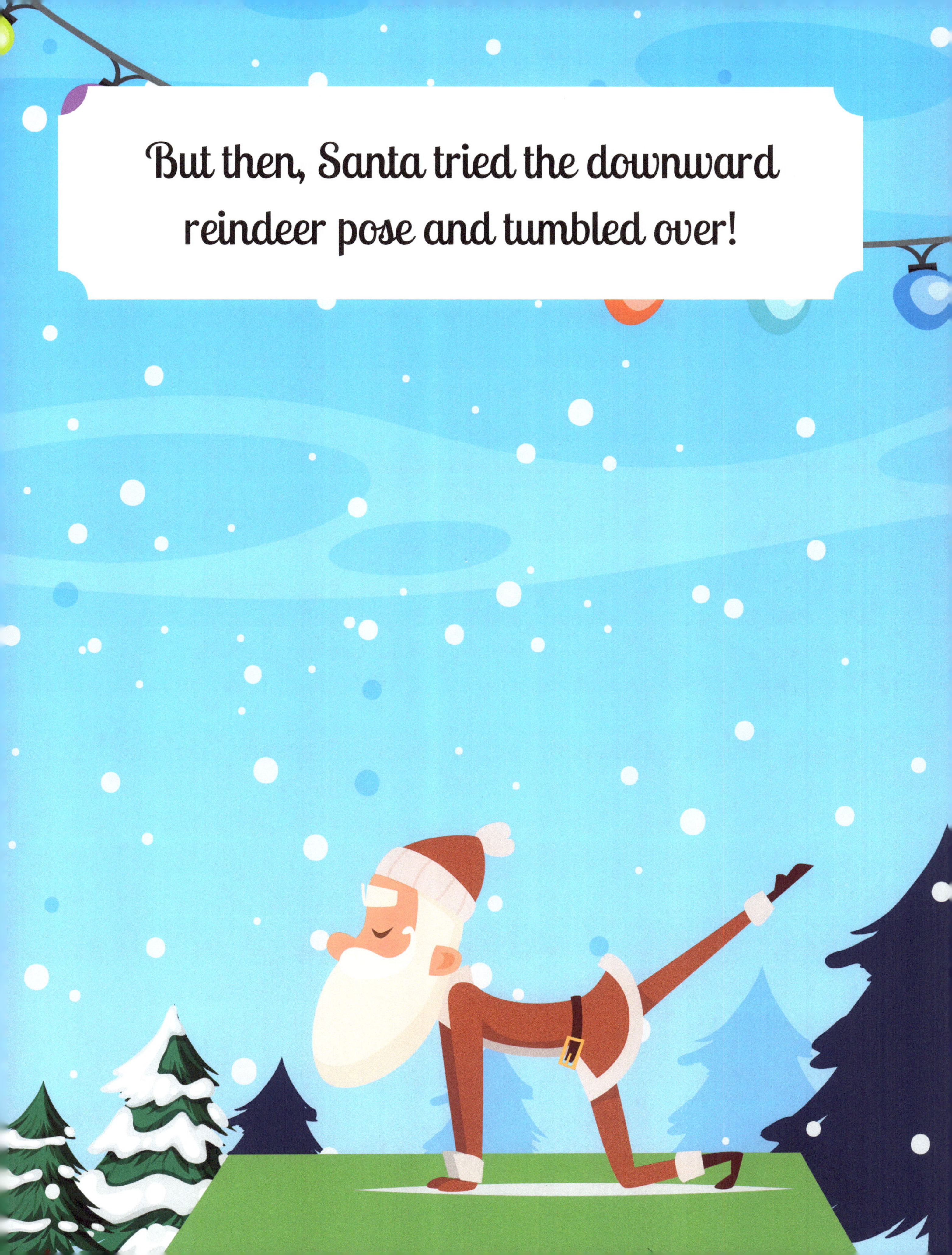
But then, Santa tried the downward reindeer pose and tumbled over!

"Oops!" Santa chuckled, "Guess I need more practice with that one!"

After finishing, Santa sat in the snowflake pose, breathing in deeply.

"Yoga makes me feel calm and strong, just what I need tonight."

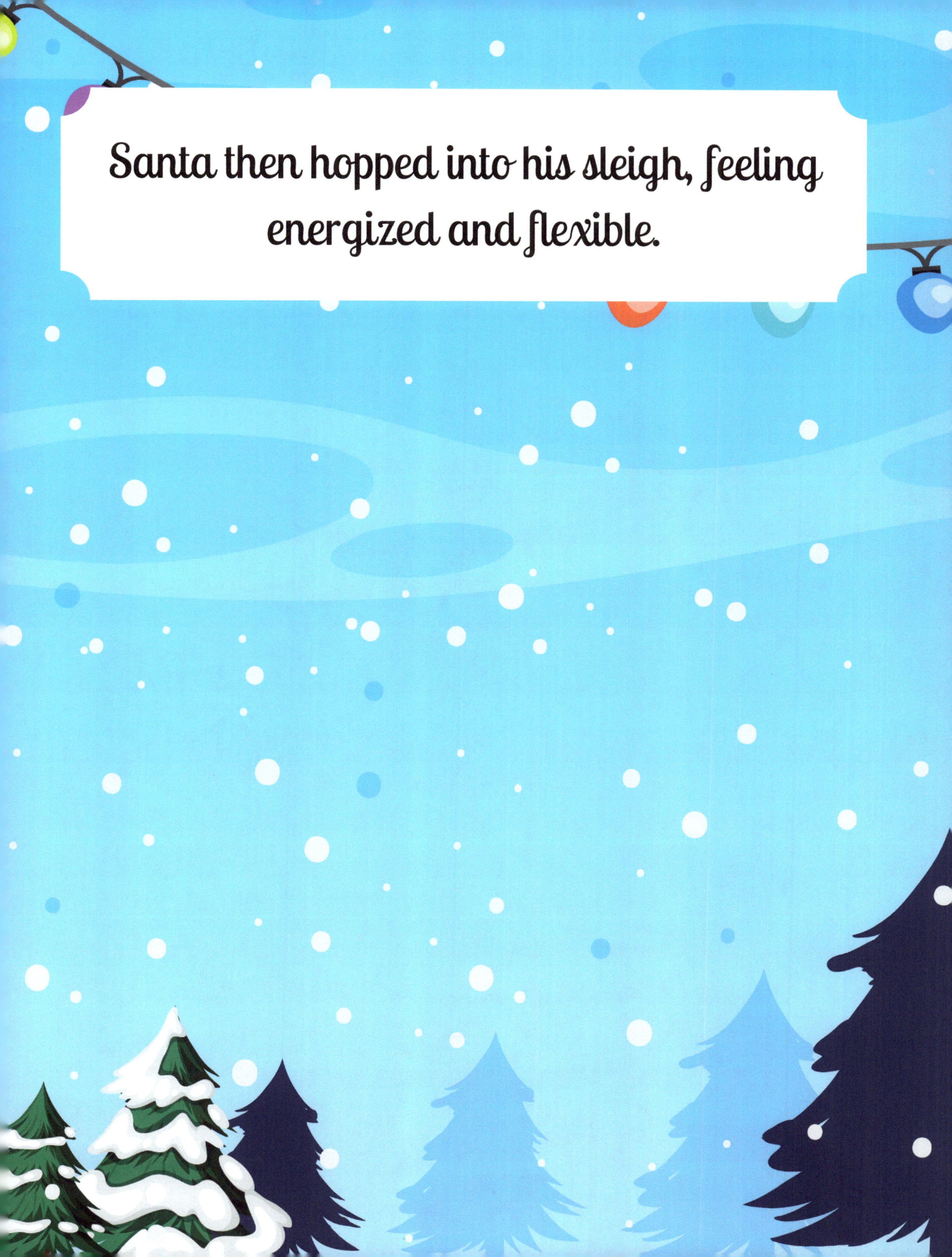

Santa then hopped into his sleigh, feeling energized and flexible.

The reindeer galloped through the sky,
pulling Santa and his gifts.

He crouched down easily to fill stockings
and place gifts under trees.

Even climbing chimneys seemed easier after his yoga practice!

"Ho ho ho!" Santa laughed. "Yoga was the perfect idea!"

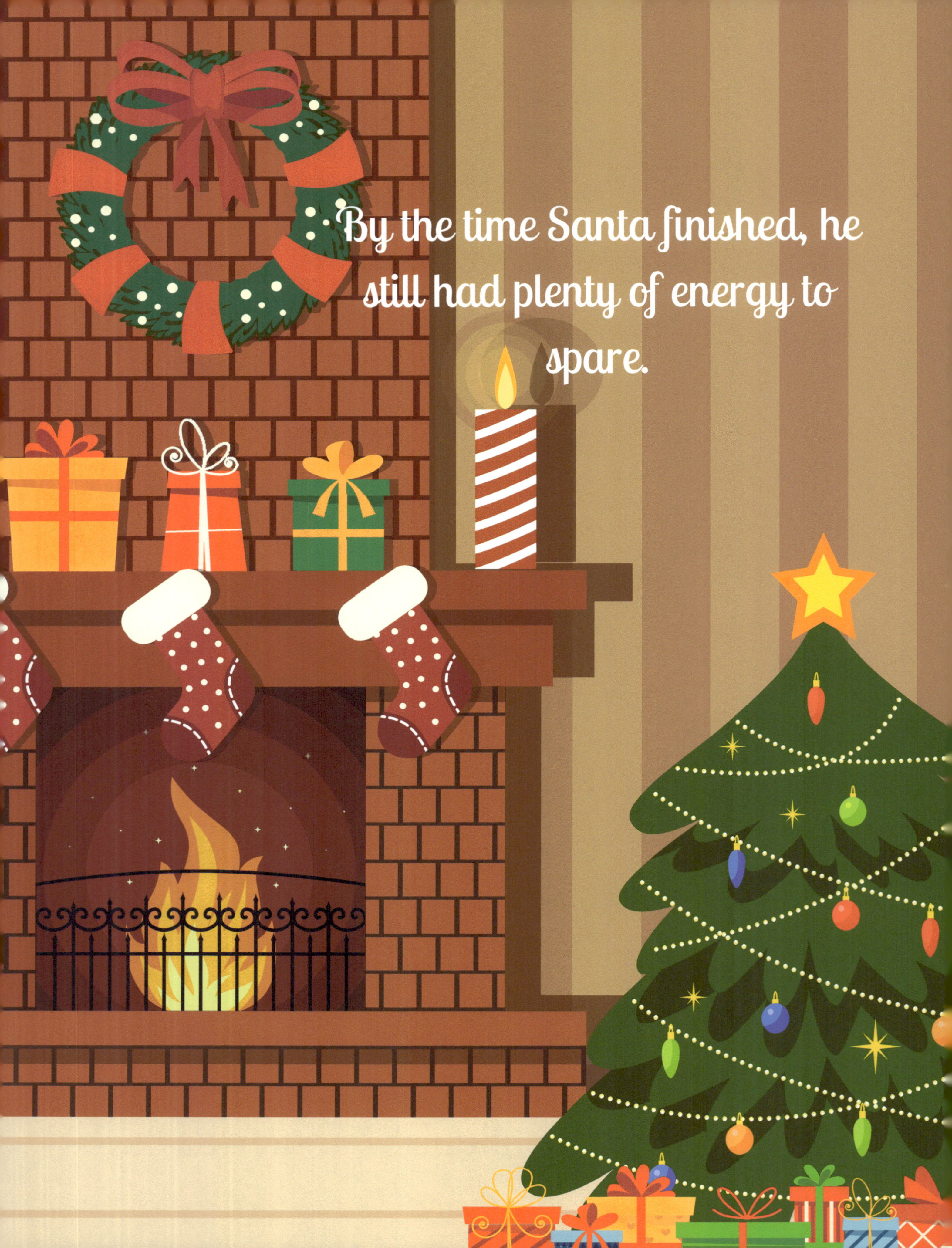

By the time Santa finished, he still had plenty of energy to spare.

He returned to the North Pole and
stretched one more time.

"I'm glad I tried yoga," Santa said. "It made Christmas even merrier!"

"Next year, I'll teach the reindeer and elves yoga too!" Santa declared.

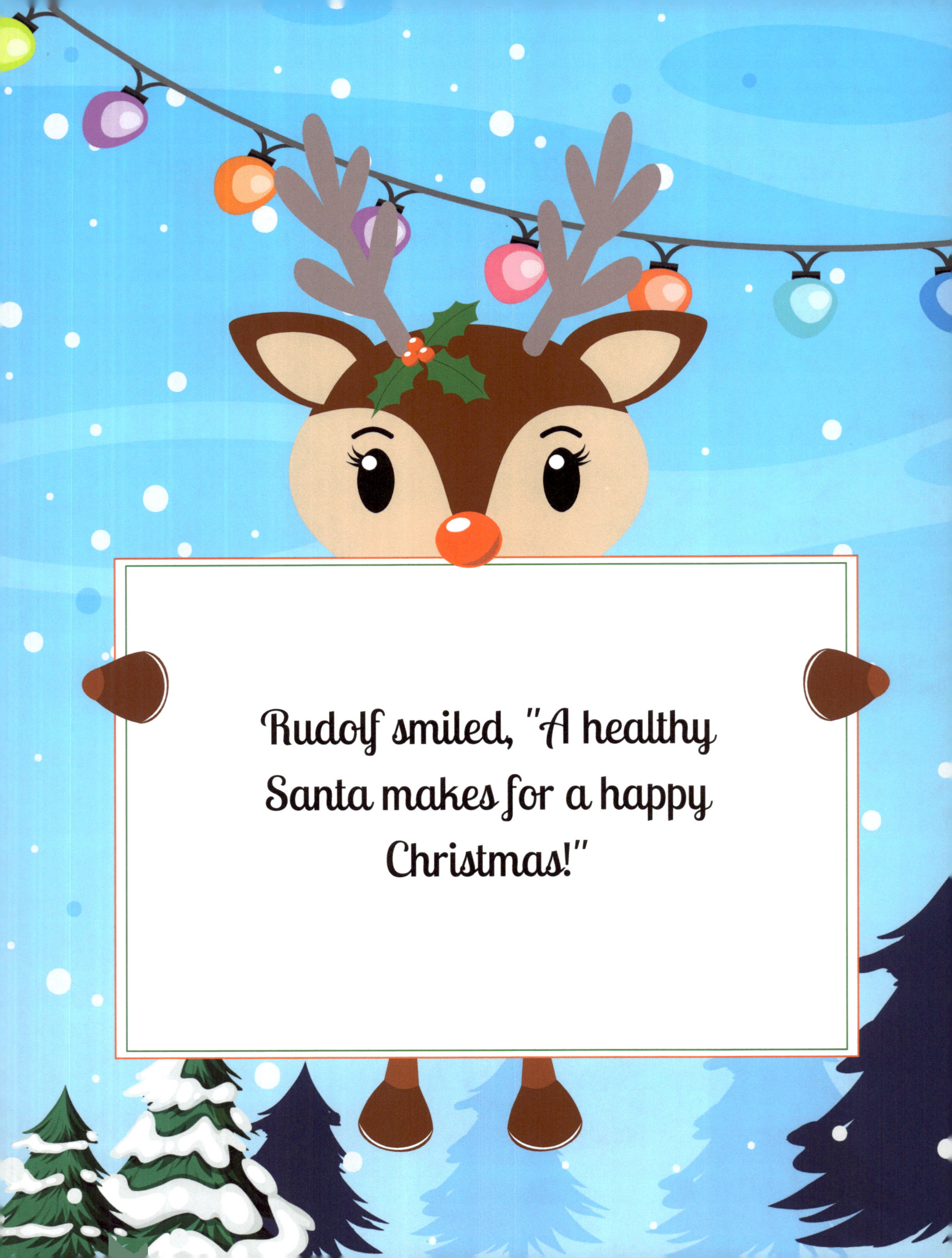
Rudolf smiled, "A healthy Santa makes for a happy Christmas!"

And from then on, Santa practiced yoga
every holiday season!

The END

Books By Schaaf

www.BookBySchaaf.com

Find us at: